Antoni Gaudí

Antoni Gaudí

Antoni Gaudí

teNeues

Editor in chief:
Paco Asensio

Archipockets coordination:
Aurora Cuito

Original texts:
Aurora Cuito and Cristina Montes

Photographs:
Pere Planells, Roger Casas,
Miquel Tres, Luis Gueilburt

English translation:
William Bain

German translation:
Martin Fischer

French translation:
Agencia Lingo Sense

Italian translation:
Raffaella Coia (Books Factory *Translations*

Proofreading:
Sabine Wagner

Graphic design / Layout:
Emma Termes Parera and Soti Mas-Bagà

Published worldwide by teNeues Publishing Group
(except Spain, Portugal and South-America):

teNeues Book Division
Kaistraße 18, 40221 Düsseldorf, Germany
Tel.: 0049-(0)211-994597-0
Fax: 0049-(0)211-994597-40

teNeues Publishing Company
16 West 22nd Street, New York, N.Y., 10010, USA
Tel.: 001-212-627-9090
Fax: 001-212-627-9511

teNeues Publishing UK Ltd.
P.O. Box 402
West Byfleet
KT14 7ZF
Tel.: 0044-1932-403509
Fax: 0044-1932-403514

teNeues France S.A.R.L.
4, rue de Valence
75005 Paris, France
Tel.: 0033-1-5576-6205
Fax: 0033-1-5576-6419

www.teneues.com

Editorial project:

© 2003 LOFT Publications
Via Laietana, 32 4º Of. 92
08003 Barcelona, Spain
Tel.: 0034 932 688 088
Fax: 0034 932 687 073
e-mail: loft@loftpublications.com
www.loftpublications.com

Printed by:
Gráfica Domingo SA, Spain

September 2003

Bibliographic information published by Die Deutsche Bibliothek
Die Deutsche Bibliothek lists this publication in the Deutsche Nationalbibliogra
detailed bibliographic data is available in the Internet at http://dnb.ddb.de.

ISBN: 3-8238-4536-5

8 Casa Vicens

14 Villa Quijano–El Capricho

20 Finca Güell

26 Sagrada Família

32 Palau Güell

38 Casa Batlló

44 Theresian School

50 Casa Botines

56 Bodegues Güell

60 Casa Milà

66 Crypt of the Colònia Güell

72 Park Güell

78 Chronology

Antoni Gaudí grew up in Camp de Tarragona, a rocky region defined by plantations of grapes, olives, and carobs. The constant observation of the landscape of his childhood and his architecture studies at the university of Barcelona led him to a particular conception of the world: that setting, with its animals and plants, brought together all of the constructive and structural laws that architects needed to plan their buildings.

Thus, the inspiration Gaudí required to make up for the few deficiencies of his genius he found in the natural world. It is not strange that under such an idiosyncratic view of his métier, Gaudí lived only to plan, forgetting the family, social, and cultural life that was going on around him.

Simplicity, immediacy of contemplation of nature to solve architectural problems made Gaudí mistrust complex mathematical calculations—he opted instead for empirical methods of checking. This procedure led him to carry out a number of experiments to calculate the loads of a structure or the final form of an ornamental device.

Gaudí's breakthroughs also stem from the imaginative treatment of materials. A good example are the wrought iron structures that are to be found in the whole of his work. The use of wood meant still another meeting point uniting this architecture and the artisans of the period to whom Gaudí went to turn his imaginative designs into reality.

Antoni Gaudí wuchs in einer kargen Gegend auf dem Land in der Nähe von Tarragona auf, wo vor allem Wein, Oliven- und Johannisbrotbäume angebaut werden. Durch die aufmerksame Beobachtung der Landschaft während seiner Kindheit und sein Architekturstudium an der Universität von Barcelona entwickelte er seine eigene Weltsicht: In der Umwelt mit ihren Tieren und Pflanzen fand er alle Gesetze der Baukunst und Statik, die er als Architekt brauchte, um seine Gebäude errichten zu können.

In seiner Genialität ließ sich Gaudí von der Natur anregen. Es überrascht nicht, dass ein Künstler mit einer solchen Berufsauffassung ein zurückgezogenes Leben führte; die Familie und die gesellschaftlichen und kulturellen Kontakte mussten hinter der Arbeit zurückstehen.

Die Einfachheit und Unmittelbarkeit, mit der Gaudí in der Natur schon die Lösungen für bautechnische Probleme vorfand, machten ihn misstrauisch gegenüber komplizierten mathematischen Berechnungen. Er zog die empirische Überprüfung seiner Entwürfe vor und stellte zahlreiche Experimente an, um die Traglast einer Struktur zu berechnen oder die endgültige Form eines Schmuckelements zu bestimmen.

Gaudís Meisterschaft zeigt sich auch beim eigenwilligen Einsatz der Materialien. Ein gutes Beispiel dafür sind die schmiedeeisernen Verzierungen, die all seine Werke zieren. Aber auch beim Einsatz von Holz konnte sich Gaudí darauf verlassen, dass die damaligen Kunsthandwerker selbst seine ausgefallensten Gestaltungsideen umzusetzen wussten.

Antoni Gaudí a grandi au Camp de Tarragona, une zone pierreuse plantée de vignes, d'oliviers et de caroubiers. L'observation continuelle du paysage de son enfance et ses études d'architecture à l'université de Barcelone lui ont donné une conception particulière du monde : l'environnement, avec sa flore et sa faune, réunissait toutes les lois architecturales et structurelles nécessaires à un architecte pour projeter ses constructions.

C'est dans la nature que Gaudí trouvait l'inspiration dont il avait besoin pour suppléer les rares déficiences de son génie. Il est peu surprenant que, sous de telles auspices conceptuelles envers son métier, Gaudí vécut uniquement pour projeter, oubliant la vie familiale, sociale et culturelle l'entourant.

La simplicité, l'immédiateté de la contemplation de la nature pour résoudre des questions architecturales le faisaient se méfier des calculs mathématiques complexes, ses vérifications demeurant empiriques. Cette méthode l'amena à réaliser de nombreuses expériences afin de calculer les charges d'une structure ou la forme finale d'une ornementation.

Le génie de Gaudí naît également du traitement imaginatif réservé aux matériaux. Les filigranes en fer forgé apparaissant dans toute l'œuvre de Gaudí en sont un bon exemple. L'utilisation du bois a signifié un autre point de rencontre avec les artisans de l'époque, auprès desquels Gaudí se rendait pour transformer en réalité les purs produits de son imagination.

Antoni Gaudí crebbe in provincia di Tarragona, in una zona pietrosa coltivata a vigneti, olivi e carrubi. La costante osservazione del paesaggio della sua infanzia i la sua istruzione di architettura a la università di Barcellona lo portò a maturare una concezione del mondo particolare, secondo la quale l'ambiente, con i suoi animali e le sue piante, aveva in sé tutte le leggi costruttive e strutturali delle quali un architetto aveva bisogno per progettare i propri edifici.

Gaudí trovò nella natura l'ispirazione che cercava per compensare le poche deficienze della sua genialità. Non è affatto strano che, con un simile concetto della propria professione, Gaudí vivesse praticamente solo per lavorare ai suoi progetti, trascurando la vita familiare, sociale e culturale che lo circondava.

La semplicità e l'immediatezza che riscontrava osservando la natura per la soluzione dei problemi architettonici rendeva Gaudí scettico riguardo i complicati calcoli matematici e per questo motivo preferiva realizzare accertamenti empirici. Questo metodo lo portò a eseguire numerosi esperimenti per calcolare i carichi di una struttura o l'aspetto definitivo di una decorazione.

La genialità di Gaudí risiedette anche nell'immaginazione applicata alla lavorazione dei materiali e ne sono un esempio le filigrane in ferro battuto che appaiono in tutta la sua opera. L'impiego del legno rappresentò un altro punto in comune con gli artigiani dell'epoca, ai quali Gaudí si rivolgeva affinchè convertissero in realtà i suoi disegni più fantasiosi.

Casa Vicens

Carolines 24-26, Barcelona, Spain
1883–1888

In 1883, the young Gaudí set out on one of his first commissions as an architect. The result still shows the straight lines he would later abandon in favor of curves and fantastic forms. But the Gaudí trademark is undeniably present in this ostentatious and singular building. The piece in question is a powerful edifice and mixes Spanish architectural forms, inspired on the medieval period, with elements of marked Arabic influence, more in keeping with Mudejar art than with the buildings of Gaudí's time, which were highly influenced by the French school. In spite of the fact that the edifice had to be built on a rather small plot and would go up between traditional buildings, what Gaudí created was a singularity perfectly adapted to its environment. The architect conceived it as a subtle combination of geometrical masses skillfully resolved via the use of horizontal borders at the lower part of the base in conjunction with the vertical lines, accentuated by the ornamentation in glazed ceramics in the upper part. The exterior walls are in simple materials such as natural stone of an ochre color combined with ordinary brick.

Im Jahre 1883 erhielt der junge Gaudí einen seiner ersten Aufträge als Architekt. Bei der Casa Vicens finden sich noch Geraden, während Gaudí später nur noch geschwungene Linien aller Art einsetzte. Trotzdem ist der Kern der Kunstauffassung Gaudís auch in diesem ungewöhnlich prachtvollen Privathaus schon erkennbar. Die Casa Vicens erscheint als ein eindrucksvoller Bau, der Elemente der spanischen Architektur, vor allem des Mittelalters, mit eindeutig arabischen Anleihen verbindet. Das Ergebnis in einer Art Mudejar-Stil unterscheidet sich völlig von anderen Gebäuden der damaligen Zeit, in der französische Einflüsse vorherrschten. Obwohl das Haus zwischen vorhandenen Gebäuden in traditionellem Stil auf einem eher kleinen Grundstück errichtet werden musste, gelang es Gaudí, einen Bau zu entwerfen, der sich hervorragend in seine Umgebung einfügt. Der Architekt erdachte eine subtile Kombination verschiedener geometrischer Formen, wobei er die Fassade im unteren Bereich durch waagerechte Schmuckbänder gliederte, im oberen dagegen durch senkrechte Strukturen aus Keramik. Diese Zierelemente kommen vor den schlichten Außenmauern aus ockerfarbenem Naturstein und Backstein besonders gut zur Geltung.

En 1883, un jeune Gaudí affrontait une de ses premières commandes comme architecte. Cette œuvre permet encore d'apprécier les lignes droites qu'il abandonnerait, plus tard, pour les courbes et les formes fantastiques. Mais le germe gaudien est présent dans cette construction singulière et ostentatoire. La maison Vicens s'affiche comme un édifice superbe, mêlant les formes architecturales espagnoles, inspirées de l'époque médiévale, à des éléments aux réminiscences arabes marquées, propres de l'art mudéjar et non des constructions du moment, sous l'influence de l'école française. Bien qu'elle ait dû être construite sur un terrain aux dimensions limitées et être encadrée par des immeubles traditionnels, Gaudí créa une maison singulière, parfaitement adaptée à son environnement. L'architecte la conçut comme une combinaison subtile de volumes géométriques, résolue habilement par l'emploi de franges horizontales pour la partie inférieure de l'édifice et de lignes verticales, accentuées par l'ornementation en céramique vernie, pour la partie supérieure. Des matériaux simples furent retenus pour les murs extérieurs, ainsi l'ocre de la pierre naturelle alliée à la brique.

Nel 1883 il giovane Gaudí intraprese uno dei suoi primi incarichi come architetto. Malgrado in quest'opera sia ancora possibile osservare le linee rette che l'artista abbandonò in seguito sostituendole con linee curve e forme fantastice, l'impronta di Gaudí è senza alcun dubbio già presente in questo sontuoso e peculiare edificio. La Casa Vicens si presenta come una prodigiosa edificazione nella quale sono fuse forme architettoniche spagnole, ispirate all'epoca medievale, ed elementi con forti reminiscenze arabe, più tipiche dell'arte mudejar che non delle costruzioni dell'epoca, nelle quali la scuola francese imponeva i propri modelli. Nonostante l'edificio sia stato innalzato su un terreno esiguo, circondato da costruzioni tradizionali, Gaudí ideò una casa singolare, ma perfettamente in armonia con l'ambiente circostante. L'architetto la concepì come una sofisticata combinazione di volumi geometrici, realizzata abilmente con strisce orizzontali nella parte inferiore dell'edificio e linee verticali, accentuate dagli ornamenti di ceramica smaltata, nella parte superiore. Per i muri esterni decise di impiegare materiali semplici, come la pietra naturale color ocra alternata con mattoni.

Villa Quijano–El Capricho

Comillas, Santander, Spain
1883–1885

The "caprice" of Máximo Díaz de Quijano to have a country residence that would adapt to the needs of bachelor life has given Villa Quijano the nickname of "El Capricho". The little edifice is on the outskirts of Comillas (province of Santander) and rises up as a solitary structure in the middle of the plain. Curved lines dominate in this project, beginning to take on greater protagonism in relation to straight edges so that we perceive the desire to return to the creation of forms in keeping with medieval Castilian architecture with Oriental reminiscences. In spite of the inspired originality that runs through the whole structure, the Catalan architect did not overlook functionality. Special attention, therefore, is paid to the interior spatial organization: the needs of the occupant of this house are fulfilled, including adaptation to the climatic conditions of the Atlantic coast of Northern Spain via a sloped roof. The compact finished product, seated on a solid stone foundation, has ochre- and red-brick walls set off by courses of glazed ceramics that alternate relief sunflower and leaf motifs.

Der Name „El Capricho", unter dem die Villa Quijano bekannt geworden ist, erklärt sich aus einer Laune des Bauherrn Máximo Díaz de Quijano, der ein Landhaus besitzen wollte, das seinen Junggesellenansprüchen gerecht würde. Das Haus erhebt sich auf freiem Feld in der Nähe von Comillas (Provinz Santander). Bei diesem Projekt sind erstmals die geschwungenen Linien gegenüber den geraden vorherrschend und er verband abermals die Formensprache des spanischen Mittelalters mit orientalischen Reminiszenzen. Bei aller poetischen Eigenwilligkeit des Baus ließ es der Architekt nicht an Funktionalität fehlen. Besondere Aufmerksamkeit schenkte er der Raumaufteilung im Inneren, die den Bedürfnissen des Bauherrn entsprach. Das schräge Dach passt sich den klimatischen Bedingungen an der nordspanischen Atlantikküste an. Das Sockelgeschoss des kompakten Baus besteht aus Naturstein, während sich darüber rötliche und gelbliche Backsteinmauern erheben, die von waagerechten keramischen Schmuckbändern unterbrochen werden, auf denen Blätter und Sonnenblumen zu sehen sind.

L'envie de Máximo Díaz de Quijano de disposer d'une résidence à la campagne s'adaptant à ses besoins de célibataire ont fait que la Villa Quijano fut connu sous le surnom « d'El Capricho » (Le caprice). La construction, située à la périphérie de Comillas (province de Santander), s'élève isolée au milieu des champs. Ce projet affiche une dominante marquée des lignes courbes, commençant à l'emporter sur les droites. S'impose à nouveau également la volonté de conjuguer l'architecture médiévale castillane et les réminiscences orientales. Bien qu'une originalité inspirée parcoure l'ensemble de la demeure, l'architecte catalan n'a pas renoncé à la fonctionnalité. Ainsi, il a porté une attention spéciale à l'organisation spatiale intérieure pour la marier aux nécessités du propriétaire et installé, dehors, un toit incliné s'adaptant au climat du la côte atlantique du Nord de l'Espagne. La construction, compacte, assise sur une solide base de pierre, s'élève avec des murs de brique ocre et rougeâtre, perdant leur homogénéité de par les décorations d'enfilades de pièces de céramique vernies, faisant alterner les reliefs de tournesol et de feuille.

Il desiderio di Máximo Díaz de Quijano di possedere una casa in campagna adatta alla sua vita da scapolo ha dato il nome a Villa Quijano, nota infatti con il soprannome "El Capricho" (Il Capriccio). La costruzione, situata alla periferia di Comillas (in provincia di Santander), si erge, isolata, in aperta campagna. In questo progetto si nota una marcata egemonia delle linee curve che predominano su quelle rette, e si riafferma di nuovo l'intenzione di coniugare le forme tipiche dell'architettura medievale castigliana con le reminiscenze orientali. Malgrado l'originale aspetto di questa casa, non si deve pensare che l'architetto catalano abbia rinunciato alla funzionalità; difatti, Gaudí fece particolare attenzione all'organizzazione spaziale degli interni per adattare la casa alle necessità del proprietario e sistemò all'esterno una copertura in grado di adattarsi alle condizioni climatiche del litorale atlantico della Spagna del Nord. Questo compatto edificio, eretto su una solida base di pietra, fu innalzato con muri di mattoni color ocra e rossiccio la cui omogeneità è interrotta da decorazioni di ceramica smaltata con rilievi alternati di girasoli e foglie.

Finca Güell

Avinguda Pedralbes, Barcelona, Spain
1884–1887

Eusebi Güell, the main patron and mentor of Gaudí, commissioned the architect to work on a residence located between the Les Corts and Sarrià neighborhoods. In addition to rehabilitating some buildings that were already standing, Gaudí was to construct other modules and additional elements and had to design various decorative devices. The huge site has two entrances, one for pedestrian traffic, the other for carriages. These are flanked by two pavilions: the porter's lodge and the stables, joined to another area used as an equestrian ring. The porter's lodge was conceived as a pavilion divided into three masses: the main body, another which is octagonal on plan, and the two semi-detached bays, on rectangular plan. The stable area was designed as a single space on a rectangular plan with parabolic arches and vaults. Thanks to the use of trapezoidal apertures, this space receives a generous portion of natural light, intensified by the whiteness of the walls. Between the porter's lodge and the stable is a large wrought iron door that includes a sculpted dragon in this same material. This is the artisan piece crafted by the workshop of Vallet i Piqué in 1885, based on a design by Gaudí.

Eusebi Güell, der wichtigste Gönner Gaudís, beauftragte den Architekten mit der Gestaltung eines weitläufigen Grundstücks in den Vierteln Les Corts und Sarrià. Gaudí sollte dort schon bestehende Gebäude umbauen und zusätzliche Bauten errichten sowie verschiedene Verschönerungsmaßnahmen durchführen. Der Zugang zum großzügigen Anwesen erfolgt über zwei Eingangstore – eines für Fußgänger, das andere für Gespanne –, die von zwei Pavillons flankiert werden: dem Pförtnerhaus und den Pferdeställen, an die sich eine Reithalle anschließt. Das Pförtnerhaus setzt sich aus drei Bauteilen zusammen: dem achteckigen Hauptbau und zwei daran angefügte Nebengebäude auf rechteckigem Grundriss. Die Pferdeställe sind als ein einheitlicher Raum angelegt, der von Backsteingewölben über weiten Bögen überspannt wird. Das durch die hochliegenden Fenster einfallende Licht wird durch die weißen Wände noch verstärkt. Zwischen dem Pförtnerhaus und den Ställen befindet sich das große Eingangstor aus Schmiedeeisen mit einer eingearbeiteten Drachenskulptur. Es wurde 1885 von den Kunstschmieden der Werkstatt Vallet i Piqué nach Gaudís Entwürfen angefertigt.

Eusebi Güell, le principal mécène de Gaudí, le chargea des travaux d'une résidence située entre les quartiers de Les Corts et Sarrià. Outre la réhabilitation d'immeubles existants, Gaudí devait construire d'autres modules et éléments additionnels et concevoir divers compléments décoratifs. Le vaste terrain comporte deux portes d'entrées – une pour les personnes, l'autre pour les attelages – et est flanqué de deux pavillons : la loge du concierge et les écuries, communiquant avec un autre lieu servant de piste équestre. La conciergerie a été pensée comme un pavillon distribué en trois corps : le principal, un niveau octogonal, et les deux volumes adossés, des niveaux rectangulaires. Pour leur part, les écuries se dessinent comme un espace unitaire de niveau rectangulaire aux arches paraboliques et aux voûtes couvertes. Grâce à l'emploi d'ouvertures trapézoïdales, elles disposent d'une lumière abondante, accentuée par la blancheur de murs. La grande porte de fer forgé, présentant la sculpture de dragon, se trouve entre la conciergerie et les étables. Il s'agit d'une œuvre artisanale créée par l'atelier Vallet i Piqué en 1885, sur une ébauche de Gaudí.

Eusebi Güell, il più importante mecenate di Gaudí, commissionò all'architetto i lavori di una proprietà situata tra i quartieri di Les Corts e di Sarrià. Oltre a ristrutturare alcuni edifici già esistenti, Gaudí avrebbe dovuto costruire ulteriori moduli ed elementi aggiuntivi e avrebbe dovuto progettare vari complementi decorativi. La grande proprietà dispone di due porte d'ingresso – una per le persone ed un'altra per le vetture – ed è affiancata da due padiglioni: l'abitacolo del custode e le scuderie, comunicanti con un altro locale adibito a maneggio. La portineria venne concepita come un padiglione articolato in tre corpi: il principale, di pianta ottagonale, e due volumi addossati, di pianta rettangolare. Le scuderie, invece, progettate come uno spazio unico di pianta rettangolare con archi parabolici e volte murate con aperture trapezoidali, dispongono di un'abbondante illuminazione, accentuata dal colore bianco dei muri. Tra la portineria e le scuderie si trova una grande porta di ferro battuto con la scultura di un drago. Si tratta di un'opera artigianale realizzata dala officina Vallet i Piqué nel 1885 sul modello di un disegno di Gaudí.

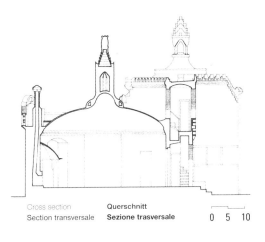

Cross section   Querschnitt
Section transversale   **Sezione trasversale**   0 5 10

grada Família

a de la Sagrada Família, Barcelona, Spain
3–1926

77, the congregation of the devout of Saint Joseph began the project to construct a large temple financed by donations. rchitect Francisco de Paula del Villar designed a neo-Gothic church but then abandoned supervision of the works. Joan rell, director of the board, recommended the young Gaudí who, at 31, took on responsibility for the work. In 1884, he d the elevation and the cross section of the altar for the Saint Joseph chapel. Gaudí imagined a church with numerous ical innovations on a plan in the form of a Latin cross superimposed on the initial crypt. The main altar was surrounded ven chapels dedicated to the seven sins and seven sorrows of Saint Joseph. The transept doors were dedicated to the on and the Nativity, and the main façade to the Gloria. On each façade four towers were planned, a total of twelve, to rep- t the apostles. The representation of Christ would be on another tower, and around this four others dedicated to the four jelists and one to the Virgin Mary. Gaudí did not finish the project which end is due in 2007.

hre 1877 begann die Kongregation der frommen Brüder des Heiligen Josefs den Bau einer großen, allein durch denmittel finanzierten Kirche. Der Architekt Francisco de Paula del Villar entwarf ein neugotisches Gotteshaus, gab h die Bauleitung ab. Joan Martorell, der Vorsitzende des Ausschusses, empfahl den jungen Gaudí, der sich dann im von nur 31 Jahren der Fortführung der Bauarbeiten annahm. 1884 legte er die Entwurfszeichnung für den Aufriss den Querschnitt des Altars der Kapelle des Heiligen Josefs vor. Gaudí plante beim Bau der Kirche, die auf einem driss in Form eines lateinischen Kreuzes errichtet werden sollte, eine Reihe technischer Neuerungen ein. Über der vorhandenen Krypta errichtete er den Hauptaltar, der von sieben Kapellen umgeben ist, die den Schmerzen und en des Heiligen Josefs entsprechen. Die Portale der Querhausarme sind Christi Geburt und Passion gewidmet, das tportal der Herrlichkeit Gottes. Jede der drei Fassaden wird von vier Türmen bekrönt, die zusammen die zwölf Apos- mbolisieren. Der große Mittelturm steht für Christus, die darum angeordneten vier weiteren Türme für die Evangelis- nd schließlich ist ein Turm für die Muttergottes vorgesehen. Gaudí konnte das Projekt nicht abschließen, die Fertig- ng ist im Jahre 2007 vorgesehen.

77, la congrégation des fidèles de Saint Joseph a lancé le projet de construction d'un grand temple financé par lonations. L'architecte Francisco de Paula del Villar conçut une église néogothique mais abandonna la direction ravaux. Joan Martorell, directeur du conseil, recommanda alors le jeune Gaudí, reprenant les rênes à seulement s. En 1884, il signe l'élévation et la section de l'autel de la chapelle Saint Joseph. Gaudí imagine une église aux reuses innovations techniques, au niveau en forme de croix latine superposée à la crypte initiale. Par dessus, l'au- incipal est entouré de sept chapelles dédiées aux douleurs et aux péchés de Saint Joseph. Les portes de la croi- u transept ont été dédiées à la Passion et à la Nativité, la façade principale à la Gloire. Sur chaque façade ont été es quatre tours, douze au total, représentant les apôtres. Une tour au centre, celle du Christ, autour de laquelle e autres tours ont été disposées pour les évangélistes et une pour la Vierge. Gaudí n'a pas finit le projet, que se nera le 2007.

877 la congregazione dei devoti di San Giuseppe intraprese la costruzione di un grande tempio finanziato attra- donazioni. L'architetto Francisco de Paula del Villar aveva progettato una chiesa neogotica, ma rinunciò alla ione dei lavori. Joan Martorell, il direttore del consiglio, raccomandò il giovane Gaudí che, a soli trentun'anni, ne responsabile dell'opera. Nel 1884 firmò il prospetto e la sezione trasversale dell'altare della cappella di San ppe. Gaudí concepì una chiesa ricca di innovazioni tecniche, con la pianta a croce latina sovrapposta alla crip- ziale, al di sopra, l'altare maggiore sarebbe stato circondato da sette cappelle consacrate ai dolori ed ai pecca- San Giuseppe. Le porte della crociera furono dedicate alla Passione e alla Nascita, e la facciata principale alla a. Come coronamento di ogni facciata furono progettate quattro torri, dodici in totale in onore degli apostoli, nel o un'altra torre rappresentante Gesù Cristo ed intorno alla quale avrebbero dovuto ergersene altre quattro dedi- agli evangelisti ed una alla Madonna. Gaudí non terminò il progetto, la cui conclusione è prevista nel 2007.

Palau Güell

Nou de la Rambla 3-5, Barcelona, Spain
1886–1888

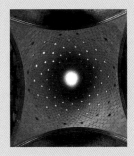

The Güell Palace, a UNESCO World Heritage building, is the work that brought Gaudí to fame. The architect designed this residence without stinting on materials and in fact with an unlimited budget. In the construction the finest stones were used, and the highest quality wrought iron and cabinetry, which made the house the most expensive of its age. The location of this urban palace on a narrow street in the Old City of Barcelona makes it impossible to see the whole structure from the outside. Güell decided to site his residence there for two reasons: in order not to abandon the family properties and to reverse the area's bad reputation. The plain stone façade does little, however, to indicate the majesty of the interior, where Gaudí unveiled an unprecedented luxury. More than 25 designs preceded the definitive building front, which was resolved on the basis of striking historicist lines and subtle classical features. The two large entranceways are in the form of parabolic arches. The four-story building has a basement and a terrace, the former accessed by two ramps, one for the service entrance and the other for the horses.

Der Palau Güell gehört zu den von der UNESCO zum Weltkulturerbe erklärten Bauten Gaudís in Barcelona. Mit diesem Gebäude machte sich der Architekt endgültig einen Namen. Gaudí hatte freie Hand, dem Budget waren keine Grenzen gesetzt. Es wurden ausgesuchte Natursteine und das beste geschmiedete Eisen verwendet und nur die besten Kunsttischler waren dort beschäftigt, so dass dieses Stadtpalais zum teuersten Gebäude seiner Zeit wurde. Der Palau Güell liegt in einer schmalen Seitenstraße in der Altstadt von Barcelona, daher ist es nicht möglich, die Gesamtheit des Baus von der Straße aus zu erfassen. Güell ließ sich sein Haus an dieser Stelle erbauen, weil er den Besitz der Familie nicht aufgeben und zudem den schlechten Ruf der Gegend verbessern wollte. Die eher nüchterne Steinfassade lässt die unerhörte Prachtentfaltung im Innern kaum erahnen. Mehr als 25 Entwürfe musste Gaudí seinem Bauherrn vorlegen, bis über die endgültige Fassadengestaltung mit ihren kräftigen historisierenden Linien und den subtilen klassizistischen Anklängen entschieden war. Durch zwei Parabelbögen gelangt man in das Gebäude, das aus einem Keller, vier Geschossen und einer Dachterrasse besteht. Gaudí legte zwei Rampen in den Keller an, eine für die Dienstboten und eine für die Pferde.

Déclaré patrimoine de l'humanité par l'UNESCO, le Palau Güell permis à Gaudí d'abandonner l'anonymat. L'architecte conçut cette résidence sans économies de moyen et sans limite budgétaire. Sa construction requit les meilleures pierres, le meilleur fer forgé et la meilleure ébénisterie, la maison se convertissant en l'édifice le plus cher de l'époque. L'emplacement du palais urbain, une rue étroite du centre historique de Barcelone, ne permet pas de contempler l'ensemble de l'œuvre de l'extérieur. Güell décida de fixer là sa résidence à deux fins : ne pas abandonner les propriétés Familiales et tenter de changer la mauvaise réputation de l'endroit. La sobriété de la façade de pierre ne laisse pas présager la majesté des intérieurs, où Gaudí put déployer un luxe sans précédent. Plus de 25 designs ont précédé la façade définitive, résolue au moyen de lignes historicistes définitives et de subtils airs classiques. Deux grandes portes en arcs paraboliques forment l'entrée de l'immeuble, doté d'une cave, de quatre étages et d'une terrasse sur le toit. Gaudí créa deux rampes pour l'accès à la cave, l'une pour le service et l'autre pour les chevaux.

Dichiarato patrimonio dell'umanità dall'UNESCO, il Palau Güell è l'edificio che rese famoso Gaudí. L'architetto progettò questa casa senza risparmiare sui mezzi e senza limite di preventivo. Per la costruzione vennero impiegate le migliori pietre, il miglior ferro battuto e i migliori lavori di ebanisteria, a tal punto che questa casa fu l'edificio più caro dell'epoca. L'ubicazione di questo palazzo, situato in un'angusta via del centro storico di Barcellona, ci impedisce di osservare dall'esterno tutta la costruzione. Güell decise di fissare qui la propria residenza per non abbandonare la proprietà della famiglia e per cercare di cambiare la pessima reputazione del luogo. L'austera facciata di pietra non fa presagire affatto la maestosità dell'interno, nel quale Gaudí spiegò un lusso inaudito. Più di 25 disegni precedettero la facciata definitiva, che venne realizzata con linee decisamente storiciste e una certa aria classica. Due grandi porte con arco parabolico costituiscono l'ingresso dell'edificio che dispone di un sotterraneo, quattro piani e una terrazza. Per scendere nei sotterranei Gaudí progettò due rampe, una per la servitù ed un'altra per i cavalli.

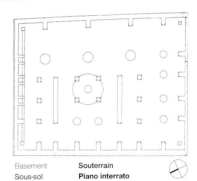

Basement   Souterrain
Sous-sol   **Piano interrato**

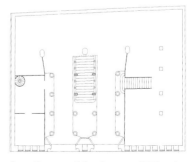

Ground floor   **Erdgeschoss**
Rez-de-chaussée   **Piano terra**   0   1   2

Casa Batlló

Passeig de Gràcia, 43, Barcelona, Spain
1904–1906

The Casa Batlló dates from 1877, and its owner, the textile manufacturer Josep Batlló, commissioned Gaudí to remodel the front and redistribute the courtyard spaces. When Pere Milà, a friend of the industrialist, learned of Batlló's plan to modernize his residence, he did not hesitate to introduce him to Gaudí, whose work Milà fervently admired. Gaudí may have been working here with an already extant building, but he still found ways to make the project a very personal one that would bear the stamp of his unmistakable style. The sensitivity of the composition is immediately appreciable from the building's exterior, which is covered in Marés stone and colored glass fragments on the first stories and similarly uses ceramic discs on the upper stories. While the refurbishment was underway, the architect decided on the very site what the optimal position for these pieces would be in terms of reflecting light and setting off the cladding. The masonry workers progressively installed the material in this way. Such a work method, perfecting an idea during the very construction process, reflects the great dedication of Gaudí in his projects, which he hardly ever considered finished.

Das Haus des Textilfabrikanten Josep Batlló bestand schon seit 1877. Als Pere Milà, ein Freund des Industriellen, davon hörte, dass Batlló sein Haus modernisieren lassen wollte, zögerte er nicht, ihm den von ihm sehr bewunderten Gaudí vorzustellen. Batlló beauftragte Gaudí mit der Neugestaltung der Fassade und einer Neuverteilung der Innenhöfe des Hauses. Obwohl er von einem bereits bestehenden Gebäude ausgehen musste, gelang es Gaudí, dem Projekt einen sehr persönlichen Charakter zu verleihen. Schon an der Fassade spürt man die gestalterische Sensibilität des Architekten: Gaudí verwendete Marés-Stein und Glas in den unteren Geschossen und keramische Verkleidung in den oberen. Während der Bauarbeiten bestimmte er selbst von der Straße aus die beste Anordnung der Keramikscheiben, um ihre Leuchtkraft bestmöglich zur Geltung kommen zu lassen. Die Arbeiter brachten die Schmuckelemente dann nach seinen Anweisungen an. Diese Arbeitsweise der ständigen Vervollkommnung der Ausgangsidee im Laufe der Bauarbeiten spricht für die große Hingabe, mit der Gaudí sich seinen Bauvorhaben widmete, die er so gut wie nie als abgeschlossen ansah.

La maison Batlló existait depuis 1877 et son propriétaire, le fabricant textile Josep Batlló, chargea Gaudí de la rénovation de la façade et de la redistribution des patios de lumière. Lorsque Pere Milà, ami de l'industriel, fut informé de l'idée de Batlló, moderniser sa demeure, il s'empressa de lui présenter Gaudí, dont il était fervent admirateur. Malgré le présupposé du bâtiment existant, l'architecte sut imprimer un air très personnel au projet. La sensibilité de la composition s'apprécie déjà de l'extérieur, revêtu de pierre du « Marés » et de verre aux premiers étages et de disques de céramique aux niveaux supérieurs. Au cours des travaux, l'architecte lui-même décida, depuis la rue, de la position idéale de ces pièces afin qu'elles se distinguent et brillent avec force, les ouvriers les disposant peu à peu. Cette façon de travailler, perfectionnant l'idée initiale durant la construction, reflète la grande implication de Gaudí dans ses projets, qu'il ne tenait jamais pour achevés.

La Casa Batlló esisteva fin dal 1877 ma il suo proprietario, il fabbricante di tessuti Josep Batlló, commissionò a Gaudí la ristrutturazione della facciata e la ridistribuzione dei patii interni. Quando Pere Milà, un amico dell'industriale, venne a sapere dell'intenzione di Batlló di modernizzare la sua abitazione, non esitò a presentargli Gaudí, del quale era un fervido ammiratore. Malgrado abbia lavorato su una costruzione già esistente, l'architetto seppe infondere uno stile molto personale a questo progetto. La sensibilità compositiva si distingue fin dall'esterno che venne rivestito con pietra di Marés e vetro sui primi piani, e con dischi di ceramica in quelli superiori. Durante i lavori l'architetto in persona decideva, dalla strada, la collocazione ottimale di ogni pezzo affinché tutti gli elementi risaltassero e brillassero in tutto il loro splendore, e gli operai li disponevano gradualmente. Questo modo di lavorare, perfezionando l'idea iniziale durante il processo di costruzione, mostra la profonda dedicazione di Gaudí ai suoi progetti che quasi mai considerava terminati.

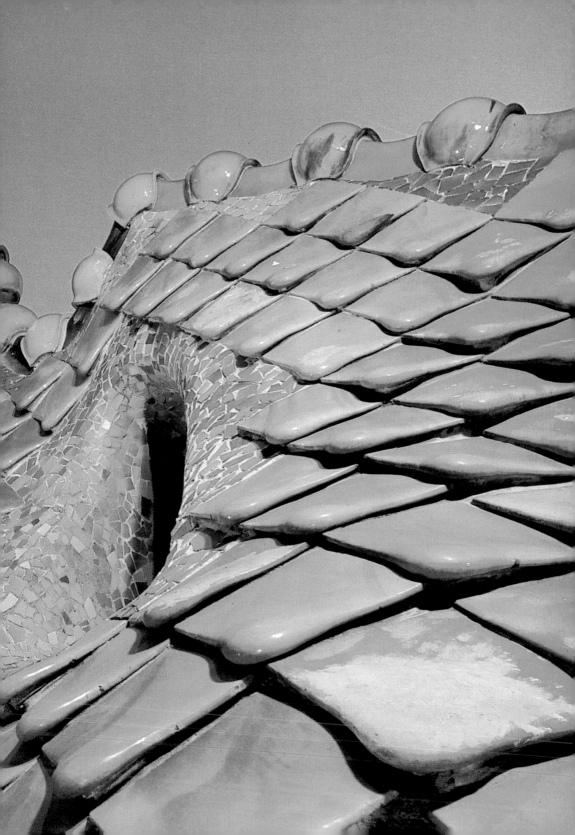

Theresian School

Ganduxer 85, Barcelona, Spain
1888–1889

Some factors, such as the rule of poverty followed by this Carmelite community, or the fact that the building would be dedicated to Saint Theresa irremediably marked the manner of designing this school in the Sant Gervasi neighborhood. The initial work, which in principle foresaw the construction of a set of three buildings, was that of another architect, and not until March 1889 did Gaudí take over the project. This meant that the ground and first floors of the building were already up when the change was made. Gaudí adapted himself to the budget—not high, compared with what was established in other projects—and to the directives set out by the previous architect (some sections could not be altered). He also accepted the austerity, asceticism, and plainness required by this ecclesiastical order. Thus, without abandoning his own characteristically unique and imaginative style, Gaudí executed a particular exercise of containment and created a project to raise an edifice of striking lines and content. Here it is moderation, absent in his previous work, that takes on the role of main protagonist, in any case in the forms, since the building is also very full of symbolic elements.

Dieses Haus für die Karmeliterinnen befindet sich im heutigen Stadtteil Sant Gervasi und ist der Heiligen Theresa gewidmet. Beim Entwurf musste auch auf das Armutsgelübde des Ordens Rücksicht genommen werden. Bevor Gaudí im März 1889 die Bauleitung übernahm, hatte ein anderer Architekt bereits mit dem Bau eines von drei geplanten Gebäuden des Kollegs begonnen, so dass Gaudí beim Erdgeschoss und dem ersten Stockwerk kaum noch Veränderungen vornehmen konnte. Er passte sich daher dem – im Vergleich zu anderen seiner Bauten eher bescheidenen – Kostenrahmen und den schon von seinem Vorgänger festgelegten Leitlinien an. Außerdem galt es die vom Orden vorgeschriebene nüchterne, asketische Strenge zu respektieren. Ohne auf seinen charakteristischen fantasievollen Stil zu verzichten, übte Gaudí Zurückhaltung und entwarf ein maßvolles Gebäude mit kraftvoller gebundener Linienführung. Ganz anders als bei seinen vorhergehenden Bauten ist die Mäßigung hier allgegenwärtig – jedenfalls was die Form angeht, denn im Grunde genommen handelt es sich um ein Gebäude voller symbolischer Elemente.

Certaines conditions, ainsi la règle de pauvreté de cette communauté de Carmélites ou la consécration de cet édifice à Sainte Thérèse, ont marqué irrémédiablement la façon de concevoir cette école du quartier de Sant Gervasi. Les travaux initiaux, prévoyant à l'origine la construction d'un ensemble de trois bâtiments, furent confiés à un autre architecte, jusqu'à ce qu'en mars 1889 Gaudí assume le projet. Le rez-de-chaussée et le premier niveau étaient donc, de fait, déjà déterminés. Gaudí s'adapta au budget – plutôt limité comparé à ses autres œuvres – et aux directives définies par le précédent architecte – certaines parties ne purent être modifiées – mais aussi à l'austérité, l'ascétisme et la sobriété requis par cette congrégation. Sans abandonner le style singulier et imaginatif le caractérisant, Gaudí effectua un exercice particulier, tout de retenue, pour projeter un édifice aux traits affirmés mais contenus. C'est la modération, absente de ses travaux précédents, qui tient la vedette. Au moins formellement, le fond de la construction fourmillant d'éléments symboliques.

Alcuni fattori condizionanti, come la regola della povertà alla quale questa comunità carmelitana ubbidiva, e il fatto che l'edificio fosse dedicato a Santa Teresa, segnarono irrimediabilmente il progetto di questo collegio situato nel quartiere di Sant Gervasi. I lavori iniziali, che prevedevano in un primo momento la costruzione di un complesso costituito da tre edifici, vennero eseguiti da un altro architetto finchè, nel marzo del 1889, Gaudí assunse la direzione del progetto, trovandosi davanti il progetto piano terra e il primo piano dell'edificio già belli e fatti. Gaudí si adattò al preventivo – piuttosto esiguo se paragonato a quello di cui disponeva per altre opere – e alle linee direttrici impostate dall'autore precedente – non fu possibile modificare alcuni elementi – , come anche all'austerità, all'ascetismo e alla sobrietà che quest'ordine ecclesiastico esigeva. Pur senza abbandonare il suo singolare e fantasioso stile così caratteristico, Gaudí effettuò un particolare sforzo di contenimento e progettò un edificio dalle linee decise ma contenute. La misura, del tutto assente nelle opere precedenti, è la protagonista almeno nelle forme, giacchè in fondo l'edificio è pieno di elementi simbolici.

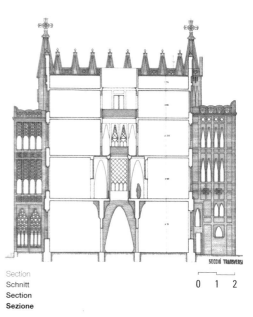

Section
Schnitt
Section
Sezione

SECCIÓ TRANSVERSI

0   1   2

Casa Botines

Plaza de San Marcelo, León, Spain
1892–1893

While Gaudí was completing the work on the Episcopal Palace of Astorga, Eusebi Güell, his friend and patron, recommended him for the construction of a house in the center of León. Simón Fernández and Mariano Andrés, the owners of a company that purchased textiles from Eusebi Güell, commissioned Gaudí to construct a residence building with a warehouse. The architect desired to render homage to the emblematic buildings of the city of León and thus designed a structure with medieval lines and a number of neo-Gothic features. The work consists of four stories, a basement, and a garret. A sloped roof was decided on, and towers were built on the corners, thus considerably reinforcing the neo-Gothic cut of the project. To ventilate and illuminate the basement, a moat was created before two of the façades (a strategy that would be repeated in the Sagrada Família). On the first floor, the owners' residences were established, accessible by independent doors in the side and back façades. The upper-level apartments were used as rented rooms and the ground floor served as the company's offices.

Während Gaudí die Arbeiten am Bischofspalast von Astorga abschloss, empfahl ihn sein Freund und Mäzen Eusebi Güell an seine Geschäftspartner in León weiter. Simón Fernández und Mariano Andrés waren Eigentümer eines Unternehmens, dem Güell Stoffe verkaufte. Sie erteilten Gaudí den Auftrag für ein Wohn- und Lagerhaus. Der Architekt wollte eine Hommage an die hervorragenden Bauten der Stadt schaffen und entwarf daher ein Gebäude mit mittelalterlichen Anklängen und vielen neugotischen Elementen. Das Bauwerk besteht aus Keller, vier Geschossen und Dachboden. Das schräge Dach mit seinen vier Ecktürmchen unterstreicht den neugotischen Eindruck. Zur Belüftung und Beleuchtung des Untergeschosses wurde an zwei Seiten des Gebäudes ein Graben angelegt; eine Lösung, die Gaudí später auch bei der Sagrada Família anwenden sollte. Im ersten Stock liegen die Wohnungen der Bauherrn, die über von einander unabhängige Türen an den Seiten- und Rückfassaden verfügen. In den oberen Stockwerken befinden sich Mietwohnungen und im Erdgeschoss sind die Geschäftsräume des Unternehmens untergebracht.

Alors que Gaudí terminait les travaux du Palais épiscopal d'Astorga, Eusebi Güell, son ami et mécène, le recommanda pour ériger une maison au centre de la province de León. Simón Fernández et Mariano Andrés, propriétaires d'une entreprise achetant ses tissus à Eusebi Güell, commandèrent à Gaudí une résidence dotée d'un entrepôt. L'architecte souhaitait rendre hommage aux édifices emblématiques du León et conçut alors une œuvre aux airs médiévistes et aux nombreux emprunts néogothiques. La construction comportait quatre niveaux, une cave et un grenier. Le choix se porta sur une toiture inclinée, dotée de tourelles aux angles, renforçant considérablement l'aspect néogothique du projet. Afin de ventiler et d'illuminer la cave, les deux façades furent ceintes d'une fosse, un stratagème répété pour la Sagrada Família. Le premier accueillait les résidences des propriétaires, accessibles par des portes indépendantes des façades latérale et postérieure. Les étages supérieurs abritaient des logements en location et le rez-de-chaussée les bureaux de l'entreprise.

Mentre Gaudí finiva i lavori del Palazzo Episcopale di Astorga, Eusebi Güell, suo amico e mecenate, lo raccomandò per la costruzione di una casa nel centro di León. Simón Fernández e Mariano Andrés, proprietari di una ditta che comprava tessuti da Eusebi Güell, commissionarono a Gaudí un edificio di abitazioni con un magazzino. L'architetto, volendo rendere omaggio alle costruzioni emblematiche di León, progettò un edificio dall'aspetto medievale, ma con numerosi elementi neogotici, costituito da quattro piani, un sotterraneo e una soffitta, con una copertura inclinata e torrioni agli angoli che ne rinforzarono notevolmente l'aspetto neogotico. Per la ventilazione e l'illuminazione dei sotterranei venne creato un fossato tutt'intorno alle facciate, uno stratagemma a cui si ricorse anche per la Sagrada Família. Al primo piano vennero progettate le abitazioni dei proprietari, nelle quali si entrava attraverso porte indipendenti situate lungo le facciate laterali e quella posteriore. I piani superiori ospitavano le abitazioni in affitto mentre il pianterreno venne destinato agli uffici della ditta.

Bodegues Güell

Carretera C-246, Barcelona, Spain
1895

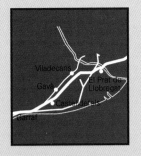

Eusebi Güell again placed his confidence in Gaudí to carry out a project on one of his estates south of Barcelona. At first the client wanted to create a project for a hunting lodge, but he then changed his mind in favor of wine cellars. Güell dedicated the land around the site to vine growing and wine production. The plantation was preceded by terracing the property to level the steep slopes of the zone. The whole comprised two buildings, the entrance lodge and the cellars themselves. The former includes a large iron door made up of a forged crossbar and the thick chains that hang from it. The load-bearing walls combine stone and brick. This blend of materials is not actually structurally necessary, but Gaudí used it to decorate façades which would otherwise have remained too rough. A large archway crowned by a mirador-balcony receives the visitor and houses the porter's lodge. The wine cellars are in a striking but austere building. Made of stone from nearby quarries, it is in fact not unreminiscent of military architecture.

Eusebi Güell vertraute Gaudí ein weiteres Projekt an. Ursprünglich wollte er sich auf einem Grundstück in Meeresnähe südlich von Barcelona ein Jagdhaus bauen. Doch dann besann er sich eines anderen und beauftragte den Architekten damit, einen Weinkeller zu entwerfen, denn er hatte das abschüssige Gelände an der Steilküste terrassieren und mit Weinreben bepflanzen lassen. Der Komplex besteht aus zwei Gebäuden: dem Eingangspavillon und der eigentlichen Kellerei. Bei den Mauern des Pavillons kombinierte Gaudí aus rein ästhetischen Gründen Bruchstein und Ziegel. Wenn das große eiserne Tor mit Querbalken und daran hängenden schweren Ketten geöffnet wird, gelangen die Besucher unter einem großen Bogen hindurch auf das Gelände. Die Pförtnerwohnung verfügt über einen Balkon als Ausguck. Der Weinkeller ist als nüchterner, trutziger Bau angelegt, der etwas an eine Ritterburg erinnert. Zu seiner Errichtung wurde Material aus nahegelegenen Steinbrüchen verwendet.

Eusebi Güell confia à nouveau à Gaudí le projet d'une de ses résidences, située au sud de Barcelone. Le client fit projeter, en un premier temps, un pavillon de chasse qui deviendrait plus tard une cave à vin. Güell consacrait les terrains environnants à la viticulture. La plantation fut précédée par une terrassement de la propriété afin de niveler les falaises escarpées de la zone. L'ensemble comporte deux corps de bâtiment, le pavillon d'entrée et les caves. Le premier inclut une grande porte de fer formée par une traverse de forge et de grosses chaînes. Les murs porteurs combinent la pierre et la brique. Cette conjonction de matériaux n'est pas nécessaire à la structure mais Gaudí décorait ainsi des façades qui auraient été, autrement, trop grossières. Un grand arc couronné par un balcon en point de vue reçoit les visiteurs et accueille la porte de la conciergerie. Les caves occupent un bâtiment austère et imposant, aux réminiscences architecturales militaires et construit à l'aide de pierres provenant des carrières voisines.

Eusebi Güell affidò ancora una volta a Gaudí il progetto di una delle sue proprietà, situata a sud di Barcellona. In un primo momento il cliente ordinò la progettazione di un padiglione da caccia, ma in seguito cambiò idea e si decise per una cantina. Güell adibì il terreno circostante alla coltivazione di vigneti per la produzione di vino. La piantagione venne preceduta da lavori di livellamento allo scopo di appianare le ripide scarpate della zona. Il complesso è costituito da due costruzioni, il padiglione d'ingresso e i cantine. Il primo include una grande porta in ferro realizzata con una traversa di metallo alla quale sono appese possenti catene. I muri portanti sono in pietra e mattoni. Quest'unione di materiali diversi non era strutturalmente necessaria, ma permetteva a Gaudí la decorazione delle facciate che sarebbero state, altrimenti, troppo ordinarie. Un grande arco, sormontato da un balcone panoramico, e al di sotto del quale si trova la porta della casa del custode, riceve i visitatori. I cantine si trovano in un edificio austero e squadrato, con reminiscenze dell'architettura militare, costruito con pietra estratta dalle vicine cave.

Casa Milà

Passeig de Gràcia 92, Barcelona, Spain
1906–1910

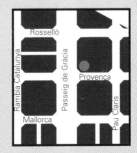

The Casa Milà rises up like a great rocky massif and, from the moment of its building, Barcelonans have called it "la Pedrera" (quarry). The project came out of the commission given the architect by Pere Milà and his wife, and it was Gaudí's last project in the field of civil architecture because soon afterwards he secluded himself to work in the atelier on the site of the Sagrada Família. Gaudí's Marian fervor led him to imagine a large edifice crowned by a bronze sculpture with the image of the Virgin. But while this was finally not included, the "Pedrera" still conserves some religious inscriptions. Gaudí conceived a system to save on materials. First, he substituted the load-bearing walls by a system of beams and columns, taking care down to the last detail with the joints in order to be able to reduce their size in section. Next, he thought up a façade that was heavy in appearance but in fact made up of thin plates of limestone. The undulant forms of the fronts, so often compared with the waves of the ocean, have correspondences inside the building, where right angles disappear: there are no irremovable walls and the detail work is calculated down to the last millimeter.

Die Casa Milà erhebt sich wie eine mächtige Felsformation an der Straßenecke, daher war sie schon während der Bauzeit als „la Pedrera" (Steinbruch) bekannt. Pere Milà und seine Frau erteilten Gaudí den Auftrag für sein letztes weltliches Bauvorhaben. Der Architekt widmete sich in den nachfolgenden Jahren mit all seiner Kraft der Sagrada Família. In seiner tiefen Marienverehrung hatte Gaudí eine bronzene Statue der Muttergottes zur Bekrönung der Fassade der Casa Milà vorgesehen, die aber nicht aufgestellt wurde. Allerdings finden sich an der Fassade einige religiöse Inschriften. Gaudí ersann ein System zur Materialeinsparung. Er ersetzte die tragenden Wände durch Pfeiler und Tragbalken, deren Verbindungen er eingehend untersuchte, um ihre Stärke auf ein Minimum reduzieren zu können. Die schwer wirkende Fassade besteht in Wahrheit aus dünnen Kalksteinplatten. Ihre geschwungenen Formen, die oft mit den Wellen des Meeres verglichen wurden, finden ihre Fortsetzung im Inneren, wo es keine rechten Winkel und keine fest eingebauten Trennwände gibt. Gaudí hat alles bis ins kleinste Detail bedacht.

La maison Milà s'élève comme une grande formation rocheuse. C'est pourquoi, dès sa construction, les Barcelonais la surnommèrent « la Pedrera » (la Carrière). Le projet naît de la commande de Pere Milà et de son épouse à l'architecte, pour sa dernière œuvre civile. Gaudí se retira en effet ensuite dans l'atelier de travail de la Sagrada Família. Sa ferveur mariste l'amena à concevoir un grand édifice couronné d'une sculpture de bronze à l'image de la Vierge. Bien qu'elle fut finalement abandonnée, « la Pedrera » conserve cependant quelques inscriptions religieuses. Gaudí pensa un système économe en matériaux. En premier lieu, il substitua aux murs porteurs un système de poutres principales et de piliers, dont il contrôla le détail des entrelacements afin d'en réduire la section. Il conçut aussi une façade apparemment pesante mais formée en fait de fines plaques de pierre calcaire. Les formes sinueuses de la façade, si souvent rapprochées de la houle marine, ont leur pendant à l'intérieur, où disparaît tout angle droit, dépourvu de cloisons inamovibles et aux détails millimétrés.

La Casa Milà si innalza come una grande formazione rocciosa, e per questo motivo, fin dalla sua costruzione, gli abitanti di Barcellona la soprannominarono "La Pedrera" (La Pietraia). Il progetto fu commissionato da Pere Milà e sua moglie all'architetto, e fu la sua ultima opera civile, giacchè in seguito si rinchiuse a lavorare nel cantiere della Sagrada Família. La sua fede mariana gli ispirò un grande edificio sormontato da una scultura in bronzo con l'immagine di Maria e, anche se alla fine la statua non vi fu collocata, "la Pedrera" ancora conserva alcune iscrizioni religiose. Gaudí ideò un sistema per il risparmio dei materiali. Innanzitutto, sostituì i muri maestri con una struttura di travi portanti e pilastri, occupandosi della loro giunzione fin nei più piccoli particolari per poterne ridurre la sezione. Inoltre, creò una facciata apparentemente "pesante", ma costituita in realtà da sottili lastre di pietra calcarea. Le forme sinuose della facciata, spesso paragonate alle onde del mare, hanno corrispondenza all'interno, dove non esistono angoli retti, né tramezzi fissi, e i particolari sono disegnati minuziosamente.

Crypt of the Colònia Güell

Santa Coloma de Cervelló, Spain
1908–1916

The crypt of the Colònia Güell is one of the most uniquely designed and interesting of the creations of Gaudí, even in spite of its unfinished nature. The architect gave nearly ten years to studying its design, although only the mausoleum in the church was actually built. The design that was presented was one of a complex enclosure, with constant references to nature. Indeed, the church itself, which was to be sited atop a low hill, would have been camouflaged within the natural environment. It was an aim that would have been achieved by using organic forms and a carefully studied polychromy, the dark tones of the mausoleum bricks mimicking the trunks of the surrounding trees, and the walls of the church rising up first in green—again to copy trees—and then in blues or whites, thus taking on the aspect of sky or cloud patches. For Gaudí this singular chromatic option not only represented nature, it also symbolized the way of Christian life. The design took advantage of the evident difference in grade to include a mausoleum with a portico and a chapel. Finally, however, only the mausoleum was built, on a star-shaped ground plan.

Die unvollendete Kirche der Colònia Güell gehört zu den originellsten und interessantesten Bauten Gaudís. Der Architekt arbeitete fast zehn Jahre lang an den Entwürfen, auch wenn schließlich nur die Krypta fertiggestellt wurde. Die Kirche sollte auf einer kleinen Anhöhe entstehen und mit der natürlichen Umgebung verschmelzen. Gaudí plante organische Formen und eine ausgeklügelte Farbgebung. So sollte der dunkle Backstein der Pfeiler der Krypta an Baumstämme erinnern. Die Mauern der Kirche sollten im unteren Bereich in grünlichen Tönen gehalten sein, um wie Baumwipfel zu erscheinen, und dann weiter oben in blaue und weiße Töne übergehen, um auf den Himmel und die Wolken anzuspielen. Diese einzigartige Farbgebung verweist nach Gaudís Vorstellungen nicht nur auf die Natur, sondern versinnbildlicht auch den christlichen Lebensweg. Der Architekt nutzte für die Krypta mit ihrer Vorhalle und der Kapelle geschickt das Gefälle des Geländes aus. Im Grundriss stellt sich die Krypta als Stern dar.

La Colònia Güell est une des œuvres les plus originales et intéressantes de Gaudí, bien qu'un projet inachevé. L'architecte consacra presque dix ans à sont étude, bien qu'il dut se limiter à construire la crypte de l'église. Un ensemble complexe fut conçu, aux constantes références à la nature. De fait, l'église, qui devait se situer sur une petite colline, se serait confondue avec le décor naturel. Cet objectif était atteint en employant des formes organiques et une polychromie étudiée, pour laquelle les tons obscurs des briques de la crypte devaient se fondre avec les troncs des arbres. Les murs de l'église devaient arborer tout d'abord une tonalité verdâtre – s'apparentant aux arbres – pour devenir bleus ou blancs, se camouflant dans le ciel et les nuages. Pour Gaudí, cette option chromatique singulière non seulement représentait la nature mais symbolisait aussi le cheminement de la vie chrétienne. Le design mettait à profit le dénivelé prononcé du terrain pour inclure une crypte avec un portique et une chapelle. Finalement, seule la crypte, au plan en forme étoilée, vit le jour.

Malgrado si tratti di un progetto incompiuto, la Colònia Güell è una delle opere più originali ed interessanti di Gaudí. L'architetto vi dedicò quasi dieci anni, ma alla fine riuscì a costruire solo la cripta della chiesa. L'artista progettò un complicato complesso con frequenti riferimenti alla natura. Difatti la chiesa, che avrebbe dovuto trovarsi su una collina, si sarebbe mimetizzata con l'ambiente naturale. Gaudí avrebbe voluto raggiungere quest'obiettivo utilizzando forme organiche ed una studiata policromia, grazie alla quale le tonalità scure dei mattoni della cripta si sarebbero dovute mimetizzare con il tronco degli alberi ed i muri della chiesa avrebbero dovuto avere prima una tonalità verdastra – simile agli alberi – per poi diventare azzurri e bianchi, confondendosi con il cielo e le nuvole. Per Gaudí questa singolare scelta cromatica avrebbe non solo rappresentato la natura, ma anche il percorso della vita cristiana. Gaudí approfittò dell'accentuato dislivello del terreno per progettare una cripta con un portico e una cappella. Alla fine venne costruita solo la cripta, la cui pianta ha la forma di una stella.

Sketch   Skizze
Esquisse **Schizzo**

Park Güell

Olot s/n, Barcelona, Spain
1900–1914

Eusebi Güell had in mind a new model of English city garden when he decided to urbanize some terrains of his in the Gràcia neighborhood. His friend and protegé Antoni Gaudí was given the commission, with the end in mind of creating a residential space near the city, one that would attract the Catalan upper bourgeoisie. As it turned out, the initiative was not as successful as foreseen. Gaudí created a project for the complex as an urbanization, which meant that the space had a perimeter wall. It was a seven-doored wall, sinuous in line, and done in bordered rubblework incrusted with ceramic fragments (a technique known as trencadís—"broken bits"). This ornamentation typology is repeated in numerous elements. Opposite the entrance, a large stairway leads to the hypostyle room—with 86 classical columns—and to the Greek theater—an esplanade above this room and delimited by a continuing bench that repeats the wavy lines. The different parts of the stairway include little islets of organic elements: one in the shape of a cave, another with a reptile's head coming out of a medallion bearing the flag of Catalonia, a third with the figure of a dragon.

Als Eusebi Güell den Entschluss fasste, ein Gelände im Stadtteil Gràcia zu erschließen, ließ er sich durch die englischen Gartenstädte inspirieren. Sein Freund Antoni Gaudí erhielt den Auftrag, in der Nähe des Stadtzentrums eine Wohnanlage für das gehobene katalanische Bürgertum zu planen. Der erwartete Erfolg blieb jedoch aus. Der von Gaudí entworfene Wohnpark ist von einer geschwungenen Mauer mit sieben Eingangstoren umgeben. Die zur Verzierung der aus Bruchsteinen errichteten Mauer verwendete Trencadís-Technik, bei der ein Mosaik aus Keramikscherben verwendet wird, findet sich an vielen anderen Stellen des Parkes wieder. Gegenüber dem Eingang führt eine zweiläufige Freitreppe hinauf zum Säulensaal mit seinen 86 klassischen Säulen. Darüber liegt das „Griechische Theater", ein großer Platz, der von einer endlosen, ebenfalls mit Keramikscherben geschmückten, schlangenförmigen Bank eingefasst wird. Auf den Treppenabsätzen sind eine Grotte, der Kopf eines Reptils, der aus einem Medaillon mit der katalanischen Fahne hervorschaut, und ein Drache zu bewundern.

Eusebi Güell avait à l'esprit le nouveau modèle de cité jardin à l'anglaise lorsque fut décidé d'urbaniser des terrains situés dans le quartier de Gràcia. Il chargea son ami et protégé Antoni Gaudí du projet avec l'intention de créer un espace résidentiel proche de la ville, attirant la haute bourgeoisie catalane, bien que l'initiative ne reçut pas finalement le succès espéré. Gaudí projeta le complexe comme une urbanisation, lui offrant dès le départ un mur d'enceinte. Celui-ci, comptant sept portes et des lignes ondulées, est réalisé en maçonnerie bordée d'incrustations de fragments de céramique (technique connue comme le « trencadís »). Cette ornementation se répète dans de nombreux éléments. Face à l'entrée, un grand escalier double conduit à la salle hypostyle – formée de 86 colonnes classiques – et au théâtre grec – une esplanade sur cette salle, délimitée par un banc continu au tracé ondulé. Les volées d'escalier sont séparées par de petits îlots aux éléments organiques : l'un en forme de caverne, l'autre en tête de reptile sortant d'un médaillon avec le drapeau catalan et un troisième figurant un dragon.

Eusebi Güell aveva in mente il nuovo modello di città giardino inglese quando decise di urbanizzare dei terreni situati nel quartiere di Gràcia. Commissionò il progetto al suo amico e favorito Antoni Gaudí con l'intenzione di creare una zona residenziale vicina alla città per attirarvi l'alta borghesia catalana, anche se alla fine quest'iniziativa non ebbe il successo sperato. Gaudí progettò questo complesso come un'urbanizzazione, e fin dall'inizio la zona dispose di un muro di cinta con sette porte e linee ondulate, realizzato in muratura a secco filettata con incrostazioni di frammenti di ceramica (tecnica nota con il nome di "trencadís"). Questo tipo di decorazione si ripete in numerosi elementi. Di fronte all'ingresso, una grande scalinata doppia porta alla sala ipostila – costituita da 86 colonne classiche – e al teatro greco – una spianata al di sopra di questa sala, percorso tutt'intorno da un sedile ininterrotto dalle linee ondulate. Le rampe della scala sono separate da piazzole con elementi organici: uno a forma di grotta, un altro con la testa di un rettile che fuoriesce da un medaglione con la bandiera della Catalogna e il terzo con la figura di un drago.

Chronology of Gaudí's works

1852	Born in Reus, Tarragona, Spain.
1867	First drawings in the magazine "El Arlequín" of Reus, Tarragona, Spain.
1867–1870	Collaborated with Josep Ribera and Eduard Toda on the restoration of the Poblet monastery, Tarragona, Spain.
1873–1878	Studies at the Escola Tècnica Superior d'Arquitectura de Barcelona, Spain.
1876	Design for the Spanish Pavilion of the Exhibition of the Centennial of Philadelphia, USA.
	School projects: patio of a Provincial Delegation and a jetty.
1877	Design of a monumental fountain for Plaça Catalunya, Barcelona, Spain.
	Plans for the Hospital General in Barcelona, Spain.
	Designed an auditorium as the final project for his degree.
1878	Design of the streetlamps for Plaça Reial.
	Store window for the glove shop of Esteban Comella, which captured the attention of Eusebi Güell, who became his patron, Barcelona, Spain.
1882	Collaborated with Josep Fontserè on the Parc de la Ciutadella. Gaudí personally designed the entrance doors and the cascade.
1878–1882	Design of La Obrera Mataronense (a textile worker's cooperative), Mataró, Spain. Plan for a kiosk for Enrique Girosi.
1879	Decoration of the pharmacy Gibert, Barcelona, Spain. (Demolished in 1895.)
1882	Design of a hunting pavilion commissioned by Eusebi Güell on the coasts of Garraf, Barcelona, Spain.
1883	Drawing of the altar for the Santo Sacramento chapel for the parochial church of Alella, Spain.
1883–1888	Casa Vicens, house for the tile manufacturer Manuel Vicens, Barcelona, Spain.
1883–1885	House for Máximo Díaz de Quijano, widely known as "El Capricho" (caprice), Comillas, Santander, Spain.
1884–1887	Pavilions of the Finca Güell (caretaker's quarters and stables), Barcelona, Spain. The pavilions now house the headquarters of the Real Càtedra Gaudí, inaugurated in 1953, belonging to the Escola Tècnica Superior d'Arquitectura de Barcelona.
1883–1926	Sagrada Família Temple, Barcelona, Spain.
1886–1888	Palau Güell, residence of Eusebi Güell and his family, Barcelona, Spain.
1887	Drawing of the Pavilion of the Transatlantic Company, at the Naval Exhibition, Cádiz, Spain.
1888–1889	Episcopal Palace in Astorga, León, Spain.

1888–1889	Theresian School, Barcelona, Spain.
1892–1893	Casa Botines, house for Simón Fernández and Mariano Andrés, León, Spain.
1895	Bodegues Güell (winery) on the coasts of Garraf, Barcelona, Spain; with the collaboration of Francesc Berenguer.
1898–1900	Casa Calvet, Barcelona, Spain.
1900–1909	House for Jaume Figueres, known as Bellesguard, Barcelona, Spain.
1900–1914	Park Güell, Barcelona, Spain; with the collaboration of Josep Maria Jujol. In 1922, it became municipal property.
1901–1902	Door and wall of the estate of Hermenegild Miralles on Passeig Manuel Girona, Barcelona, Spain.
1902	Reform of the house of the Marqués of Castelldosrius, Barcelona, Spain.
	Decoration of Café Torino, Barcelona, Spain; with the collaboration of Pere Falqués, Lluís Domènech i Montaner and Josep Puig i Cadafalch. (Not conserved.)
1903–1914	Reformation of the Cathedral of Palma de Majorca, Spain; with the collaboration of Francesc Berenguer, Joan Rubió i Bellver and Josep Maria Jujol.
1904	House project for Lluís Graner.
1904–1906	Reformation of Casa Batlló, Barcelona, Spain; with the collaboration of Josep Maria Jujol.
1906–1910	Casa Milà, widely known as "La Pedrera", Barcelona, Spain; with the collaboration of Josep Maria Jujol.
1908–1916	Crypt of the Colònia Güell, Santa Coloma de Cervelló, Spain.
1908	Gaudí received the assignment to construct a hotel in New York, which remained only a sketch.
1909–1910	Schools of the Sagrada Família Temple, Barcelona, Spain.
1910	The work of Gaudí is displayed at the Société Nationale de Beaux-Arts in París, France.
1912	Pulpits for the parochial church of Blanes, Spain.
1914	Decides to work exclusively on the Sagrada Família Temple.
1923	Studies for the chapel of the Colònia Calvet in Torelló, Barcelona, Spain.
1924	Pulpit for a church in Valencia, Spain.
1926	Gaudí is hit by a tram on June 7 and dies three days later at Hospital de la Santa Creu in Barcelona, Spain.